CW01652084

How to Win Writing Competitions (and Make Money)

Cathy Bryant

Puppywolf

Created in Manchester, UK

How to Win Writing Competitions (and Make Money)

ISBN 978-0-9565819-5-2

© 2015 Cathy Bryant

All rights reserved. Any unauthorised publishing, broadcasting, public performance, copying, recording or re-recording will constitute an infringement of copyright.

The right of Cathy Bryant to be identified as the author of this work has been asserted by him in accordance with the Copyright, Design and Patents Act 1988.

www.puppywolf.co.uk

Contents

Cathy Bryant

Cathy Bryant has won 14 literary awards, including the Bulwer-Lytton Fiction Prize in 2012. She has blogged for the Huffington Post, and her stories and poems have appeared in over 100 different publications, including *Pop-shot, The Moth, The Andromeda Spaceways Inflight Magazine* and *Futuredaze.* In 2014 her poem *The Poetry Diet* (from her first collection, *Contains Strong Language and Scenes of a Sexual Nature*) was featured on BBC Radio 4's *Poetry Please* with Roger McGough. She is one of the judges for National Flash Fiction Day's short flash fiction competition, and co-editor of three volumes of *Best of Manchester Poets.* Cathy's latest poetry collection is *Look At All the Women* (Mother's Milk), and her novel *Pride and Regicide* was recently published by Crooked Cat. She runs the Comps and Calls writer's website (www. compsandcalls.com) and lives just outside the city of Manchester, UK. Learn more at **www.cathybryant.co.uk.**

Introduction

I have been very lucky.

I've won fourteen writing competitions recently, and been runner-up in countless others. I received £300 ($457) for a poem that took me a couple of hours to research and another couple of hours to write, and $250 (£164) for a single sentence of fiction. For a 100-word story, I was sent £350 ($533) and a hamper of breakfast goodies. For a single sentence, I won a trip to Italy. Bundles and boxes of books and other prizes have weighed down my postwoman, and the publicity following one of my wins (that publicity including a radio interview to 700,000 people) sent sales of my first book soaring into profit.

Perhaps unsurprisingly I've been asked to judge some competitions and edit a few books too, which has taught me more about the best ways to submit and enter - and the worst.

Yet a few short years ago I won nothing. Not one solitary sizzling sausage.

Development

Of course, my writing has developed over those years - I hope so, anyway! - but it hasn't changed that much. What has made the difference is strategy. Over the years I've learned all sorts of useful info - info that has turned my poems and stories into prize winners. This book is all about that strategy and information - it contains everything that I wish I'd known years ago, when I used to dream of winning a writing competition, but was never placed.

It happened for me, and if you use all the information in this book then there's a good chance that it can happen for you too.

This is not a book about how to improve your writing. The chances are that you already have a shelf full of those, and if you don't you can still improve your work by workshopping it, editing it, attending classes, learning techniques, performing pieces and having them critiqued.

This is simply a book about how to use your writing to win competitions.

No entrance fees

Oh – and now you have this book, you shouldn't need to pay out another penny unless you really want to. Entrance fees? Who needs them? And as for the myth that the competitions are all won by professionals – it's nonsense. You have as good a chance as anyone else if you follow the steps in this book. Some competitions are only open to unpublished beginners, anyway.

Read on, and happy winning!

My credentials

Writing competitions won or placed in by Cathy Bryant, with what was received by way of prize or reward:

Won or placed highly:

- Winner: Marple Humorous Poetry Prize 2010 – £125 ($190)
- Winner: Swanezine poetry competition 2012
- Winner: Malahat Review Monostich Poetry Contest - book bundle

- Winner: Sampad Inspired by Tagore Poetry Prize 2012 - £300 ($457), book, dance performance of work at award ceremony
- Winner: M.R. Jordan short story competition 2013 - $50
- Winner: Plenitude Twiction Competition 2013 - subscription
- Winner: Bulwer Lytton Fiction Prize 2012 - $250 (£164)
- Winner: Punbelievable 2013 weekly
- First Place: Creative Writing Liverpool 'Winter Without Clichés' Contest 2013 - books
- Gold Award: Creative Futures Literary Award 2013 - £150 ($228) prize, £100 ($152) towards writing course, certificate, critique
- Highly Commended: Rialto/RSPB Nature Poetry Competition - huge lumps of prestige
- Winner: Writers' Forum Poetry Competition February 2014 - £100 ($152)
- Winner: Mslexia Littlems newsletter flash fiction competition - £350 ($533) and a big hamper of breakfast goodies
- First Place: Nov 2014: Pen 2 Paper Coalition of Texans with Disabilities Poetry Prize - $100 (£66)
- Winner: Vivesoy 'Perfect Moment' Contest - trip for 2 to Rome, Italy

- Winner: Watch Me Bounce Inspirational Meme Contest Dec 14 - $20 (£13)
- Winner: Riding Light Review Newsletter microfiction contest Dec 14 - free print copy and $5 (£3) Amazon gift card
- Gold Medal: UPLI Global Poetry Contest, Yukon Legacy Award - $300 (£197)
- Winner: Balticon 49 Poetry Contest 2015 - $100 (£66), souvenir book, certificate

Runner-up or commendation

- Special Commendation: 2014 Firstwriters Poetry Competition - free subscription
- Runner up: Woman & Home Short Story Contest 2009 – box of books
- Runner up: Arthritis Care Creative Writing competition – book
- Runner up: Strange Circle Fiction Contest 2011 – Amazon voucher
- 2nd place: Watch Me Bounce Contest 2012
- Commended: Rhyme & Reason Poetry Contest 2012
- Runner-up: Great Escape Contest
- Runner-up: Southbank Hayward Gallery George Condo Ekphrasis Competition
- Runner-up: SFPA Poetry Contest 2012 - choice of books

- Runner-up: Prole Laureate Competition - copy, £30 ($46)
- Runner-up: Hayden's Ferry Review Limerick Competition - copy of the magazine
- Commended: Café Writers Poetry Prize 2012 - £50 ($76)
- Commended: Poetry Pulse Competition 2013
- Commended: Portico Poetry Prize 2013 - book, award ceremony tickets
- 3rd Place: Goddess Moons Speaking of Women Competition August 2014 - Goddess Moons starter kit - reuseable sanitary towels!
- 3rd place: Rank Formsby Poetry Prize 2015 - framed print
- Bronze Medal: UPLI Global Poetry Contest, Short Free Verse - March 2015 - $100 (£66)

Chapter 1
Do not skip this. Yes, it's The Basics

Thank you for not skipping this. You have just done the single most useful thing that you can do to help you to win competitions. So many people don't bother with the basics - they assume that they know them already and do them already. Even if that turns out to be true, and you read this whole chapter and don't discover a single thing that you don't already know and do, then at least you can rest assured that you're doing this part properly. You'll know to focus your efforts on other sections of the procedure for entering writing comps. I'll tell you where to find all the free writing comps in later chapters.

But also, you can use this chapter as a checklist.

Use this chapter as a checklist

When entering any comp, use the sections below and check each one off against your current entry. Have you followed all the entry guidelines? Have you read all the Terms and Conditions? And so on. You won't have to think and remember all of these points – they'll be here for you to go through, simply and easily, before committing yourself.

There's a reason that I'm so keen to emphasise the basics, and that's because I'm pretty sure that I've forgotten, messed up or not bothered with every single one of them at least once – and I'm a professional writer. Don't waste your time as I used to, and thus waste an opportunity.

Entry requirements & submission guidelines

Read and follow the entry requirements and submission guidelines.

This is the most important, and it's the one that most people fail on – up to a third of entrants, in some cases.

This needn't be the writer's fault – sometimes the comp page will say, "Send your work A4, single spaced, with your contact details on a separate document" and that's all. But buried in the terms and conditions, or a lengthy set of rules, is another criterion: "You must send your entry in the font Garamond, in 14 point type" or something similar. Reading the main comp page, you'd have no way of knowing that - and the rules also state that any entry not conforming perfectly to the rules will be deleted unread...

The only solution is to read, or at least skim read, every single page of info about the competition on the website. This may be up to a dozen pages, but they all need at least a glance - and the rules, how-to-enter, terms and conditions and eligibility pages all need to be read and reread with close attention.

Double-check deadline and eligibility

One important thing to check is the deadline. It may say, 4th January - but when you come to your computer on 4th January, the website says 'This competition is now closed'. The reason might be that the deadline was midnight on 4th January, so you have missed the window, or it might be that the competition was hosted in a country with a different time zone to yours. Always submit the day before, just to be sure, if you can!

Eligibility is important, as this is also frequently buried in tiny print somewhere other than the main comp page. There's no point in sending your sestina, however brilliant, to a comp asking for sonnets by men over 50 if you're a woman under 30.

Shunn formatting

Sometimes a short story competition will ask for 'William Shunn'-style formatting, and then link to the long list of requirements. This will put off many potential entrants but with the assistance of my favourite tech helper I've put together a guide to help you whizz through the process using Microsoft Word. See Appendix B on page 117 and turn your piece into the perfectly-formatted entry.

Read your work out loud before sending it

You can do it by yourself in your bedroom, or in the bathroom, where no one can hear you, if you're shy. It's astonishing how often this catches a clunky line or an awkward construction, or the accidental name-change of a character. It's also, of course, extremely good practise for performances and launches. You can use a hairbrush or comb for microphone practise - keep it an inch from your mouth, not on your chest: eat an ice cream, don't let it drip on your shirt... Have fun! Even if you think it unlikely that you'll ever perform your work, enjoy the practise. And listen to yourself - which parts of the piece are working and which aren't? If you can record yourself and listen to it afterwards, all the better. Yes, I know, it's cringe-making - but it's helpful.

Proofread your work

No, a spell-checker and grammar-checker won't cut the mustard. Also to be avoided are thesaurus apps - one recently changed 'left behind' to 'sinister buttocks'. This is not likely to be helpful. As a judge myself, I've seen misuse of all these things and they are not impressive.

Proofread it again and again. And then, unless the deadline is looming, leave it for a few weeks and proof it again. If it doesn't win the comp or is rejected by the magazine then proof it again. That lapse of time can really help - you'll notice more of the errors when you have some distance from the piece. The trouble is that when you read your own work you tend to see what you meant to write rather than what you actually did write, so if you have a skilled and willing friend, get him or her to look it over too.

Proofreading: A bit more depth

The need to proofread can be annoying - what if you're dyslexic? What if you're a brilliant writer, but not that great at spelling and grammar? Maybe you weren't taught well at school.

The sad fact is that most comps will have loads of entries, and the judges simply don't have time to spend hours reading and re-reading each entry (not at the first round stage, anyway) to see if they are works of genius despite all the 'errors'. Those errors make your work more difficult and time-consuming to read, and judges (particularly first-round sifters) will simply reject them.

Please note that I'm not talking about dialect. A poem written in consistent dialect can be a joy, and full of life and vision.

Neither am I saying that such strictness is a healthy way to approach language – I'm just telling you how to win writing competitions.

At primary school we were given examples of 'bad' spelling. Personally I think that they are rather beautiful and poetic, but are they comprehensible? Do you know what they mean?

- metantatipi
- wyrntn

Me neither. It turns out that the writers meant "meat and tatie (potato) pie" and "wire and tin". The "correct" version is easier to understand.

This does not mean that you should dumb down your work and make everything simple and easy to understand, just that you should spell 'correctly' and use grammar 'correctly', unless you are writing in the voice of a character who speaks using 'bad' grammar. If you can't do these things, then enlist the help of someone who can - a friend or a teacher.

Be pleased when they find things to correct, not upset - they are helping to make your work more likely to win a prize! Great!

If money isn't an issue then you can pay a proofreading service. Try a few until you find one you are happy with.

Of course another option is to buy or borrow a book on English usage. They can be quite dense reading, but infinitely useful. If you've forgotten whether "If I were a rock star" or "If I was a rock star" is correct, then a book like that can be a great help, and second hand ones can be very cheap. I recommend Fowler's English Usage, any edition at all. In case you're wondering, "If I were a rock star" is correct - hypotheticals use the subjunctive. I don't know what that actually means and I was never taught it, but I've learned to use it properly. I don't know if blindly following a poorly-understood rule is a good thing - probably not - but I do win competitions.

Sure, you can find grammatical information and correct spellings on the internet (make certain, however, that you use American English for American competitions and UK English for UK competitions) - but do make notes (typed or handwritten, not copied-and-pasted) of what you find, at the very least. It sticks better in the mind.

I bought my Fowler's for £4, including postage. It has repaid me a hundredfold. I use the internet, too - and an old Chambers dictionary (use Oxford if you must, or Webster's for US English) and a Roget's Thesaurus, though never ever use a word from the thesaurus unless you understand it fully. An example of bad thesaurus use: "Walking round the art gallery, I was imbibed with wonder". Um - no you weren't. The writer has mistaken drunk (meaning intoxicated) for drunk (as in swallowed). It ruins the piece.

The more tools you have the better, and you will learn which suit you best, or which combination suits you for particular tasks.

One final word on proofreading: I sent my best poem out to magazine and competition after magazine and competition, and it kept getting rejected.

Then I proofread it again, and saw the typo in the first line... Corrected, it was snapped up by the next publisher to whom I submitted it.

Be a professional

This mostly translates as: be courteous. When you submit/enter, unless it states otherwise on the entry guidelines (e.g. via an internet form with no space for a cover letter) send a polite message introducing yourself and you work. NOT a bio, unless they've asked for one, and not a life story - literally, introduce yourself and no more, unless the entry/submission guidelines state otherwise.

This is my standard cover/entry letter:

Dear XXXX,
Please find attached my poem "Alas for the Shards of My Putrefying Dismay," which is my entry to your "Unworkable Clichés" Contest. Thanks for taking the time to read my work.
Yours sincerely,
Cathy Bryant

Try to use the name of the judge/editor for the 'XXXX' part. If it isn't available then use the name of the organisation/magazine.

DO NOT argue with the results of a contest, however ridiculous and unfair. If you send a message to the organisers, however reasonable and polite, then you are flagging yourself up to the organisers and judges as a discourteous amateur. Unfortunately, the literary world has its share of nonsense and dung, often combined. Don't put judges and organisations off you because you reacted inappropriately to it. Tell your closest friends, particularly your closest writer friends (but not on a public forum), and talk about it with them - let off steam in a safe and private environment only.

Do not expect to win all or many competitions, particularly at the start of your comping career. Winning writing competitions is a skill that can be learned, but it usually takes a bit of time. The judicious use of the info in this book should cut down that time greatly, but you will still have things to learn as you go along.

See Chapter 8 for instructions on what to do when you win! And now that we've got the basics sorted out, it's time to find out how to get the winning edge...

Chapter 2
Getting the edge

If you find and enter plenty of writing competitions and take care of the basics, then you have a good chance of getting prizes. There are, however, several things that you can do to improve the odds of winning.

Research

The first is research. Check the judges of the competition, if they are named. What is their work like? Incidentally, many judges say that they aren't seeking work like their own and that they want to be surprised. They aren't exactly lying, and they wouldn't be pleased by a poor imitation of one of their own works, but I've found that judges who write punchy urban verse give prizes to punchy urban verse, and judges who write King-esque horror stories give prizes to King-esque horror stories, and judges who write elegiac nature poems give prizes to elegiac nature poems, on the whole. So make sure to enter something at least vaguely within (and not opposed to) the parameters of the judges' preferences, as well as following the rules for the competition. Read previous winners of the competition by all means, but do see whether or not the same judges are being used. If the judges have changed, then their preferences are more important than the results from previous years. If the same people are judging or the judges aren't named, however, then pay very close attention to the previous winners' entries. Don't imitate but be aware of style and form.

Another way to get an edge is to check the blog or website of the judge, and read articles written by them. If they talk about the competition then they may well list their pet hates. I once read an article by a judge who declared his dislike of poems in the form: "And then you....and then I....We....". I had just written a poem (admittedly not a great one!) in this form - a person being addressed sadly by a narrator running through what they had done together. The judge had a good point, really - such poems are clichéd, and I didn't bother entering it. Instead I revised it completely, and it was eventually published in a very different (and much improved) form.

Another thing to check is whether there are sifter judges. These are people who read all the entries before passing a shortlist to the (usually more famous) judge. See if they are mentioned and named. If a competition changes its judge but not its sifter judges, and you haven't had success, then you may still not have success with the same sifter judges. Is it still worth entering? If it's free then yes - always. If it isn't, then think about it carefully.

Do not do

A few things NOT to do. Don't plagiarise. Don't plagiarise. DON'T PLAGIARISE. Yes, a few writing competition winners have been plagiarists - and have been exposed and disgraced. There may be those out there uncaught, but even if you didn't get caught - do you really want to do something that kills your writing skill, that chokes it and squeezes the life out of it? Promising and skilled writers have turned into emotionally dead whiners when they plagiarised. If you don't know what I mean then read some of their 'apologies' and other comments about plagiarism. Do you ever want to write like that? Do you want to be that person?

I know people who have won top writing competitions with prizes of many thousands of pounds. I also know people who have got six-figure publishing deals. And without exception they are thoughtful, honest, sharing people, who would NEVER steal another person's work. If you want to emulate them then work hard at your writing. We all begin with dubious first drafts and we all write pieces that aren't much good - but if you do all the smart things and persevere, then you will become a much better writer, and stand a chance of winning those prizes and getting those deals - honestly.

Research the theme

If the competition has a theme, then research that theme. For instance, if a poem about Marilyn Monroe is required, then at least read the Wikipedia page, and preferably watch one of her films or more. Take notes as you go along. What strikes you? What grabs your attention? The same goes for a short story about, say, bodysnatching. What is the history of bodysnatching? What exactly was the process? What happened if the perpetrators were caught?

Don't attempt to research and create at the same time. They are different skills and use different parts of the mind. Do your research and take your notes - you should have a page or so of stuff that interests you. It doesn't have to be the central ideas; you aren't writing an essay for school, or taking an exam. In fact peripheral information can be very useful, and your poem about the hairspray that Marilyn used or your story turning on the state of the bodysnatchers' shoes could stand out as unusual while remaining pertinent.

When you have done your research, sleep on it. Let at least one night pass before you attempt to start the writing of your piece. This time lets your unconscious mind process and play with the information you gave it, and this is when ideas can emerge. Do keep a notebook and pen, or suitable electronic device, by the bed to jot down any ideas that pop up as you are drifting off or waking up!

Then you will be ready to write your first draft. Perhaps you will already have your idea and can zoom straight into the writing. If not, no problem - the next chapter is full of ways to make that happen.

When you have written your piece, do a check on it as well as the usual proofreading.

Does it contain any clichés?

I don't mean just the obvious ones, such as 'as white as snow' or 'murky depths'. Yes, get rid of those, and substitute something more appropriate (for instance, in a school story, 'as white as paper' or 'as white as chalk' might be more appropriate, and in a zombie poem 'decaying depths' might work a little better). But make sure to get rid of what I call lazy lurkers. These are phrases that have been massively overused, but wouldn't feature in any list of phrases to avoid. Here's a few examples:

- he grinned inanely
- I feel different, somehow
- a drunken stupor
- waves crashing on the shore
- turn that frown upside down
- rhyming 'love' with 'dove'
- and with that, she walked away in the rain
- putrefying flesh

... and so on, and so on. I hope you get the idea. Have you used any lazy lurkers like these? What do you really mean? How are you picturing the scene in your mind's eye? What is your piece really trying to say? Write that instead - even if it comes out a bit clunky at first, never mind - it'll be your view, not a bad-novel-of-forty-years-ago view, and you can always edit it later. The main thing is to get rid of the lazy lurkers. Go through your work with an eye out for them.

This applies to the ideas in your piece, too. Does the world really need another poem saying that love can hurt? If so, make sure you're putting your own version of that across, or showing it in a new way. As an editor, I've also seen far too many short stories and poems that are basically an angry account of someone's faults and bad behaviour, and end with the murder of that person, usually with a knife. It's boring (and sometimes creepy in the self-indulgent-violent-fantasy way). At least give your piece something of you, something unique. I don't mean that ghastly thing, 'a unique selling point', which sounds like a cleaning product advertised on a shopping channel – I mean your own writer's voice. Stop thinking about spin and start thinking about expression. Make it your own.

Does it hang together?

Does the form fit the content? By that I mean, have you written a poem about death and misery in dull quatrains? If so, it'll be hard to pull off. Or have you written your delicate and subtle comedy of manners in monosyllabic pulp style? You may lose the nuances.

Actually odd combinations like this can work sometimes, but be aware of the relationship between form and content and try different things to see what works for each piece.

Then check each line or sentence. This sounds like hard work, but it's worth it. Is each line of your poem adding something to the piece? What would happen if you cut it? Can it be jiggled? Is each sentence of your story helping the narrative on, or adding atmosphere, or demonstrating character, or something equally useful or beautiful?

Being this rigorous with your pieces will iron out all sorts of errors and weaknesses and make them shine.

What if you change the POV (point of view)?

If the poem is in third person, why not try it in first person? If the story is in second person - hard to pull off - see if it works in third person. What about the ending? What happens if you change it? Basically, play with the piece. Save the draft you were happy with, at all costs, but copy it into a new document to play with. What if you change the location/focus/mood of the piece?

One thing - you wouldn't believe how many winning poems are set in exotic locations. I once wrote a spoof of a prizewinning poem, which didn't get published - until I moved its setting to South Africa. 'Otters Playing at Dusk While a Loved One is Ill' became 'Groot Otters' - and won me £100.

Actually submit the piece – and by the closing date!

You wouldn't believe it, but this is the one step that trips up many would-be winners. They've written the piece - they don't know whether or not it's any good - they fear that it isn't - and they talk themselves out of sending it, thus ensuring that they don't win the competition.

It's very sad not to have enough confidence.

Here's a secret: you don't need confidence; you just need to pretend that you have - and it helps to remember that no one (except the judges) will ever know that you entered the competition, and that even though there's only a small chance of winning, just entering is something of which you should be proud. You had a go! Hold your head high!

As for, "What if they hate my entry and think it's the worst they have ever seen?" - it really isn't, if you've done even a quarter of the things that I've suggested. I've been an editor and a judge, and seen poems torn out of birthday cards submitted, stories in which almost every word is misspelt and there is a cliché in every line, and poems that have clearly been sent by someone who doesn't speak English very well at all. At the worst they won't like your work much - and so what? You can be the best writer in the world and everyone won't like your work - Shakespeare has his critics, as does any other respected writer you care to name.

Enter. Write down what piece you entered and where in your Submissions document. Have a quick happy daydream about what it would be like to win. Then forget all about it and move on to the next piece.

Chapter 3
Make inspiration happen: Becoming your own muse

An awful lot of writers talk about 'the Muse', and how they only write when she descends with celestial inspiration. When I hear that I stare longingly at the bar, and excuse myself as quickly as possible before I say something impolite.

Admittedly that's an extreme response, and I do know what they mean. Sometimes inspiration strikes and you are filled with the urge – no, the need – to write down the glorious words as they come to you. The resulting piece works, and has that special quality that happens when everything comes together, as if touched by magic.

If you only write at these times, when this inspiration descends, then you won't write very often. And here's a thing - only one of the many acclaimed and prizewinning writers I know ascribes to this belief in the Muse. Yes, when you get that feeling, write! But also write when you don't get that feeling and the Muse is off on holiday somewhere, probably sunning herself in Greece or Italy. This also makes something special happen - it makes the Muse more likely to visit. In effect, if you open the door to her and put the coffee on for her and plump up a cushion on a comfy chair for her, she'll turn up more often.

What do I mean with all this metaphorification? Well, in a few words: writing exercises, word counts, workshops and routines. Keep the writing part of your mind awake and alive - practise and extend and explore your creativity - make time and room for it. If you do that, then you make it far easier for the Muse to turn up.

Exercise and time

Some people sneer at writing exercises. I see them as the equivalent of going to the gym or doing an exercise workout. You're unlikely to do anything amazing there, but when you do come to climb the mountain or enter the tennis tournament, the work you did in the gym sure helps. And sometimes records do get broken in gyms, and people have breakthroughs.

A word to those whose 'Muse' is/was a particular person - possibly an ex, or a family member who passed away. If they have gone out of your life and you have stopped writing as a result, remember that they didn't write your poems or stories - you did. They inspired them, but you were the writer capable of being inspired. If you have that capacity, you don't lose it. You will be inspired again and you will write again. In the meantime, do the exercises and keep your hand in. The person may have gone but your gifts haven't, and they are waiting for you to nurture them.

Make the time to write

Some of us like to write a particular number of words a day. A thousand is a popular number, but if your time is stretched then even a hundred is a useful daily achievement. If your days are just too chaotic then make that target weekly, or instead of a word count, write for a specific length of time. If you are still thinking that you don't have the time, well, unless you have more than one child under 3 or two jobs, then that isn't the case. You need to prioritise your writing. There are not many things as stupid as the person who says, "I could write a great novel, but I don't have the time." Finding the time is what makes novels happen. It's part of what it means - loads of us have great ideas for novels, but only a small fraction of us write them down.

Imagine if someone said, "I'd be a great parent, but I just don't have the time."

Making the time is part of what being a good parent is! Making the time to write is also part of being a good writer.

Making the time to find and enter writing competitions is part of what it takes to be a winner.

It's also a really good example to set to your children. Do you want them to fulfil themselves and be creative when they're adults? Then show them that grown-ups like you are allowed to take time to themselves, to create, express and work on their writing.

OK - lecture over!

I'm disabled with several chronic health conditions, so I can't keep to a strict routine, as some days I can't write at all. So I write whenever I can - really whenever I can. I do the tasks I have to do each day, and then I go to work - writing. I take frequent rests, and sometimes I can't write very much at all, but writing is the thing I do when I'm not doing other absolutely necessary things. If you want to be a prizewinning writer, and you have that love of writing, then I suggest that you do the same.

In terms of competitions, experience with workshop exercises comes in really handy. This is because many contests are themed. It can be really hard to write a particular number of words on a particular subject in a particular form if you aren't used to doing writing exercises and approaching them with confidence, or at least an open mind. I'm going to list ten different writing exercises/approaches to use for themed contests. Try several for each theme, and pick the best piece that results to work on for entry. One piece of important advice: do NOT try to think about polishing your writing/getting your entry ready while you are doing the exercise. Let the creative part of your mind take over and just do the exercise - judging the results comes later. If at any point a great idea comes and you want to run with it - do! This isn't school. You don't have to finish the exercise if it has already worked.

Exercise 1: Ten things

Without thinking too hard about it, write a list of the first ten things that come into mind when you heard that word. So for 'bridge' you might find yourself writing: railway, hump-backed, local, suspension, card game, teeth, troubled water, water under the bridge, bridge of sighs/size, Pont-Neuf.

Then write a few words beside each item in your list.

Take the ones you can still stand and write a five minute burst on each of them.

Try putting two of the concepts together and see what happens. For instance, during an important bridge game (say against the boss, for high stakes), a player feels her dental bridge come loose. She can't adjust it, and she can't leave the game during the hand to do so. How will she handle this? What if someone speaks to her, and she is expected to reply? This could turn into a comic story of social embarrassment, about hating one's boss and deciding to get another job when your teeth fly into your colleague's whisky glass...

Even if the ideas don't sound great, write a few of them anyway. Your creativity may well take over and make a moderately interesting idea into a well-worked one, or you may find yourself flying off on a tangent – with any luck, a useful (and saleable or prizewinning!) one.

Exercise 2: Taking away

Imagine a world in which the [insert theme of competition] has been taken away. What is the world like without it?

This can work in various ways. If the theme of the contest is 'time' for instance, what would the world be like without a sense of time – if people performed actions without a temporal framework? Would nostalgia exist? How would things like workdays function? Or is there no time itself in the world - no age or decay, but no seasons either or successive days and nights - things just are. What would that be like? Would life be perfect, or static?

Exercise 3: Memories

With the competition theme in mind, start writing a piece beginning with the words: "I remember..." This can be surprisingly powerful, even therapeutic. You can always cut out the 'I remember' afterwards if it looks clunky or clichéd (and it usually does - my advice is to cut), but never worry about things like that during the actual exercise. Keep writing for at least ten minutes, even if it's tough. If you really don't have any memories regarding the theme then try, 'I imagine...' and write as if you did. An alternative is to take a historical personage who experienced the theme (e.g. Cleopatra for beauty, Henry VIII for inconstancy) and write as if you are that person! Write their memories.

Exercise 4: Collages

If you have a few weeks until the contest deadline, and the theme is something to be found in written material (e.g. 'face', 'money', 'news') then make a collage. All you need is a piece of board - the side of an empty cereal packet will do - some Blu-Tack or similar repositional adhesive, and a pair of scissors. Then collect things such as the free local papers, flyers and other junk mail in your letter box, food containers (clean), catalogues, leaflets handed out by people on the street, and so on. Look for images and words related to the competition theme and cut them out. Doodle, draw and make notes yourself, if you can. When you have a good handful, arrange them on the board, any way that feels right. As always with workshop exercises, don't think too hard about it. When the collage feels 'done', take a night off. The next morning, as soon as is reasonable (I can't do a thing before breakfast and medicine), get the collage, look at it and write, even if you begin with just simple descriptions of what you see and how you feel about it. Readjust the collage as much as you like, though I recommend taking photos of it first so as not to lose a particular dynamic.

Exercise 5: The image event

This is for competitions with a provided photo or picture, which has to inspire the entry, though it can be adapted for any themed competition, as I'll explain.

Look at the image. Now see what it depicts as an event. What process led up to that event - what happened before? What is happening now? What will happen after the event? What processes will follow?

This works surprisingly well. Even if the image seems uninspiring - say, a dull still life of flowers in a vase - you get to decide who arranged them that way and why, and what they meant to do and couldn't. You get to decide what people thought of them, and what happened afterwards. Were they thrown at someone's spouse in a fit of rage? Did they decay slowly?

You can also find images to fit a theme using Google. Put the theme into Google (or your search engine of choice): e.g. Life on Other Planets. Then when the results come up, click on Images. There may well be some surprising (and helpful) pictures in there. Now do the exercise described above, using the image that struck you as most useful and/or appropriate.

Exercise 6: Extension/opposition

This is particularly useful for 'idea' themes such as 'The youth of today is the hope of tomorrow' (one I had to do at school and hated with every fibre of my being), or 'value' themes such as 'greed' or 'kindness'. Take the idea to extremes and write about what would happen or how you might see the world. Perhaps every single person being greedy would result in the return of slavery, for instance, or constant global war; or perhaps the youth of today is hopeless and tomorrow is doomed (not my view, but it might make an entertaining story). This tends to work well in the first person. Another plan is to take the opposite view to the one you hold and write from that point of view. For instance, write a poem about greed being an excellent quality or kindness being a waste of time. This can backfire – as education crumbles, the number of editors who can perceive and appreciate the Unreliable Narrator technique is dwindling, but it's still worth a try.

Exercise 7: Friends

No, not the TV sitcom. Instead, ask friends what the first thing is that comes into their heads when they hear the theme. I know, I know – you're a writer and you'd rather not talk to people. That's OK – ask on Facebook, or whatever form of social media you use. I'm not suggesting that you nick their ideas wholesale, of course. Use them as a jumping off point, or play with them. If a response really grabs you then ask permission to work it into a poem or story, explaining that you'll change details and identities (and make sure that you do), and develop it yourself.

If you don't use social media then ask at your next party or social event. Wait until everyone has had a glass or two of wine or beer if possible.

If you don't like to socialise, even virtually, then read forums on the subject. An awful lot of what you find will be dross, but occasionally gems lurk within the mire. Just remember – do not steal – do not plagiarise. Use ideas as prompts.

Exercise 8: Google/other search engines

Try following the theme with 'is' and see what your favourite search engine brings up. Don't press enter too soon - often the suggestions start getting interesting before you've even finished that 'is'. To see what I mean, type 'never' into your search engine and don't press return. All those suggestions - mine has 'neverwinter' which sounds like a fantasy story waiting to happen. Then try 'gold is' and again, look at the suggestions. Great, aren't they? Mine has, among others, 'gold is the new pink', 'gold island singing monsters' and 'gold is best'!

Then press Enter and look at the websites that result. Still not sure where you're going? Write a list of the suggested phrases, and the most interesting things from the websites. Start arguing with them or agreeing with them. What sort of character did the writer have?

(Note: you MUST make sure that your virus protection is up to date and your backup functioning, in case of dodgy websites).

Exercise 9: Perspectives.

A child's view of the theme, an adult's view of the theme. Or a poor person's view and a rich person's view, or an Eastern view and a Western view, or a woman's and a man's view, and so on. These don't necessarily have to be opposed - in fact your work might work better if you understand and sympathise with both and juxtapose them, getting the conflict from elsewhere. For instance, if the theme is 'the Environment' then a child might dislike dirty litter in the streets just as an adult dislikes waste dumping at sea. The two fit well together and might make an interesting comparison, as the principle is the same. The conflict, if you're writing fiction, comes from the litterbugs (individual or corporate) and the problem of what to do about them. If you write as two voices discussing the subject - perhaps one in first person and one in second or third - then you may construct an interesting poem, or find the characters for a story.

Exercise 10: Superhero

You are a superhero and you did a Great Thing with that theme. If it's 'war' then you ended all wars; if it's 'flowers' then you made all flowers grow beautifully, and on every wasteland. If it's 'food' then you took mountains of excess food to feed the hungry, and if it's 'railways' then you prevented a terrible accident. Write about the fantastic thing you did. This one is fun! Of course you could always be a Supervillain instead, and write about the way you got rid of the theme - 'love' or 'hope', and how delighted you are now that it has gone - your minions are so much more efficient at work now that they aren't distracted by lovers or friends.

In conclusion

So there you go. If you haven't written for ages then you may find these hard. Don't worry - just like physically exercising for the first time in ages, it's tough. Persevere and try another writing exercise next time your schedule says that you are going to write. Try the one that looks most fun, even if it doesn't fit the theme perfectly. Or if none of these suit you then look up other exercises - there are plenty offered free on the internet. Keep going and that fire will light inside you sooner or later, usually sooner.

I'm going to finish this chapter with a gorgeous quotation from a fine, respected writer:

"Don't loaf and invite inspiration; light out after it with a club, and if you don't get it you will nonetheless get something that looks remarkably like it."

— Jack London

Chapter 4
Double your chances

I know an awful lot of writers. Some write fiction; some write poetry. What always surprises me is how few write both.

To improve your chances of winning writing competitions, write poetry and fiction!

Before you protest, I know that many people are strongly drawn to one and not the other. You might argue that you've tried writing the other genre, and it just didn't work, and the results were awful.

How long did you try for? How many attempts did you make? Who (other than you) decided that the results weren't good?

The block is usually a psychological one, not one of skill or ability. A few writing exercises and a little practice will usually take care of the problem, as many skills are transferable from fiction to poetry and vice versa. All you have to do is to tell yourself that it might be possible, and that you'll give it a go; then do some exercises, and you're off.

Trying out poetry

It can be daunting to sit down and write a poem when you don't know how, or haven't seen a poem since the one you hated at school. I suggest reading some poetry - there's plenty free online - and see if you really find it that bad or that impenetrable. Read some Wendy Cope; read some Billy Collins; read some Sylvia Plath; read some John Clare; read some Anna Akhmatova; read some Benjamin Zephaniah; read some Ogden Nash. There may be all sorts of nuances that you don't quite get, and bits (or certain poets) that don't work for you - but is it really impenetrable or impossible to write? No.

It is hard to write good poetry - all the poets I've mentioned make it look effortless, which is part of their skill. One of my favourite books is the Collected Works of Sylvia Plath, because in it we get to see her early, less perfect work – you can see her skill evolve. Geniuses weren't born able to fashion timeless classics from their first crayonings – they had to learn. You can learn – perhaps not to be a genius who will be worshipped for eternity (though who knows?!) but very possibly to win poetry competitions.

Your first poem

Here's a suggestion for writing your first poem.

Go outside, if you can, to your garden or to a park or somewhere with bits of nature in it. If you can't, then go and sit in your kitchen/bedroom and start observing like anything. Open a window if you can. Get some vegetables or fruit out.

Write notes of everything you sense – it doesn't matter if that's 'a kingfisher just flashed down the stream' or 'my feet are really cold' or 'I can smell decaying vegetable matter'. Write it all down on separate lines.

Take it home and get it out again. What was the mood of your notes? What did you feel about the experience? Write a few things that come to mind when thinking about where you've been. Put each one on a separate line.

Now put the two sets together and pick out ones that go together, that just feel right or that form a narrative or a contrast (or for any reason you like). Write them down and then read them out loud.

How does it sound? Is there any rhythm coming through?

For instance:

'At the park
Waste of time, waste of time,
litter, bitter, fed up, crime'

… might be the start of a rhyming poem, a grumpy trudge through a dull and disappointing space.

Or:

'I'd forgotten the laughter of playgrounds.
Was I ever so easily happy?
Bright scarves everywhere
– the fun of mittens –
when did I stop wearing ketchup red?'

This is a promising start to a free verse poem about missing childhood, by the look of it.

Another exercise is this, based on one by Cynthia A. Cochran of Illinois College: write a paragraph of prose describing something – a person, place or thing, including how you feel about it and what you'd like to happen to it. Now take out all the parts that are necessary to construct sentences but don't really add to the content, e.g. determiners and articles. Read the result out loud and add in pauses where it feels right - those are your line breaks. Or read it on the page and cut into lines where it looks right.

Face it - you're writing poetry...I hope you're enjoying it! When you're comfortable doing this, try writing in a few forms. Start looking at rhythm and meter and have a good play. Using forms actually frees you up to write more poems; they aren't straitjackets but opportunities. Good ones to begin: clerihew, triolet, haiku, villanelle (you can find definitions/instructions on the internet very easily for how to write these). Practising forms helps your free verse to develop, too. Any time your writing is starting to feel a bit samey or dull, then write in an unfamiliar poetic form and see it come to life.

You are now a poet.

Starting with fiction

As for those of you who write poetry but not prose....oh come on! Don't worry if it 'turns into' poetry. There is no limit to how lyrical and poetic prose can be.

Here are a couple of writing exercises for you to try prose:

1. Write a letter from the teacher of a child who grows up to be the person you like least in the world,

to his/her parents. This teacher has a fair idea as to what this person is like already...

2. Take a narrative poem of yours and turn it into a short story. Start with the same line, but keep it going as sentences. Add to what you have, and flesh it out.

3. Write a first person ('I') account of something you've always wanted to do, but haven't - explain how you went whitewater rafting and amazed the instructors, or how you saved the life of a celebrity, who then went into publishing and brought out all your books. Write it as a diary entry, as if it happened - and make it exciting and fun.

You are now a fiction writer.

If you're really struggling with this then I suggest that you read Stevie Smith's novels. Was there ever anyone with a more poetic mindset? But see how she transfers her skills across to the novel. Ditto Sylvia Plath's short stories and novel. Her first competition win was with 'Sunday at the Mintons' - a short story, not a poem.

Don't expect miracles

Whichever discipline you've come from, don't expect the new one to come as easily as the familiar. It'll take a little time, but it'll be worth it. And the effect is to sharpen your skills, not blunt them. Notice that the list in Chapter 1 'The Basics' and the checklist in Chapter 2

'Getting the Edge' and the writing exercises in Chapter 3 'Be Your Own Inspiration' ALL apply to BOTH fiction and poetry. Writing and editing one will make you more professional at writing and editing the other.

Of course the best result from the point of view of competitions is that you can now enter twice as many - no need to leave out the prose or poetry ones. You have just doubled your chances of getting a prize.

I ought to make a confession here. When I started going to writing groups, I kept explaining that I was a short story writer, not a poet. I had no interest in or aptitude for poetry, I explained seriously. Some of the writing exercises resulted in poems, but I still wasn't a poet, I said. I built up quite a portfolio of poems in time, but still "wasn't a poet". Some got published, and I was asked to perform some, and I was still claiming not to be a poet. Eventually I began to laugh at myself, and deliberately wrote a poem about not being a poet at all...that was published in my first poetry collection, "Contains Strong Language and Scenes of a Sexual Nature".

Don't be too unconfident about your work in the 'new' genre. If you follow the list in the 'Basics' chapter - proof it, kick out the clichés and so on - then you will be turning in a professional piece of work that may take the judge's fancy. Don't forget that all-important point - actually submit it! That is more important than anything else. If you don't enter then you won't win - if you do enter, then you might.

Chapter 5
Sharpen your comp-hunting spears

Entering competitions can be great fun, especially writing competitions in which you can showcase your creativity. It's lovely to dream of the prize and the praise. But how do you go about it? Don't all competitions have expensive entry fees? Where can you find free-to-enter writing competitions, and how on earth do you make your entries likely to win?

The answers are all here.

How many writing competitions do you enter per year? Two? Ten? Twenty? That isn't enough, and all those entrance fees (if you're entering comps with entrance fees) can mount up until you're paying out large amounts of money. And which comps do you enter? If you enter the most famous and prestigious ones, then you do not help your chances of winning. Unless they're free-to-enter, so that you might as well take the chance, it probably isn't worth it until you know how to win writing competitions, and exactly what comp judges want.

This chapter is designed to help you find as many writing comps as possible - in particular the free-to-enter ones.

Are you one of the people who think that there is no point in entering the free comps, as they'll have so many entries? This isn't necessarily true. One free competition I entered had only twenty entries. My entry was the only one to follow the submission guidelines to the letter - and I won the cash prize for first place. There are often very few entries for free competitions because they are less well-known than the posh ones with big prizes. If you can find them, they are well worth entering.

The web is obviously your biggest resource, though I will later give instructions for those who don't have access to it.

There are several newsletters which list comps - sign up to them, skim-read them and focus on the free comps. Then there are the websites listing comps. Make sure to visit these at least once a month, if not more often.

Websites

Here are the most useful websites I've found that list writing competitions, though I've saved the very best one for the end of the chapter, because it's mine and I want it to stand out:

- **Prizemagic Writing Comps**:
  www.prizemagic.co.uk/html/writing_comps.htm
- **The Poetry Library**
  www.poetrylibrary.org.uk/competitions/
- **BookTrust**
  www.booktrust.org.uk/prizes/
- **Creative Writing Ink**
  http://creativewriting.ie/writing-competitions/
- **Write Jobs 500 Report**
  www.writejobs.info/search/label/free%20writing%20contests?updated-max=%22%20%22&max-results=7&start=7&by-date=false
- **Writers Reign (Short Story Competitions)**
  www.writersreign.co.uk/Short-Story-Competitions.html

- **Freelance Writing**
  www.freelancewriting.com/creative-writing-contests.php
- **WritersServices**
  www.writersservices.com/listings/writing-opportunities
- **New Pages**
  www.newpages.com/classifieds/writingcontests/
- **Mslexia**
  www.mslexia.co.uk/whatson/listings/master.php?listing=2
- **Writers Reign (Magazines for Writers)**
  www.writersreign.co.uk/Magazines-for-Writers.html
- **The Review Review**
  www.thereviewreview.net/classifieds/contests

At the time of writing, each of these has at least one free writing comp listed. Make a note of each of these that you find, listing them by date in a Word doc (or equivalent) on your computer. This document (call it '[Your Name] Writing Competition Calendar' or something similar) is now your writing schedule.

Newsletters

And here are the best newsletters to sign up to:

- **Hope Clark**
  www.fundsforwriters.com/newsletters/
  The famous Hope Clark's 'Funds for Writers' will help with all aspects of writing, and includes comp listings.

- **The Review Review**
  www.thereviewreview.net/classifieds/contests
  Click on 'Subscribe to Newsletter' at the top. Get the newsletter from The Review Review as well. It will keep you up to date with what's happening in the world of litmags (literary magazines), but getting the newsletter will also remind you to check their classifieds - competitions and calls for submission. Most of the comps they list require an entry fee, but not all. They also have excellent articles on all aspects of writing and submitting (including one by me). They also sometimes have a competition in which you can win a subscription to a litmag. It isn't a writing competition, but a multiple choice to which the answers can usually be found at the website of the prize litmag. Reading litmags can, of course, let you know what is going down well in the worlds of poetry and

fiction, but they can be expensive, so don't miss an opportunity to win one.

- **Writing Career**
  http://writingcareer.com
  Writing Career is possibly the most helpful place to find competitions that pay. Sign up to their newsletter and you'll get a weekly digest of competitions and calls for submission.

- **Duotrope and Firstwriter**
  https://duotrope.com and
  https://www.firstwriter.com
  If you can spare the cash, then subscribe to Duotrope and Firstwriter. You can get a lifetime subscription to Firstwriter for a little more than a year's subscription to Duotrope, but if you submit work to magazines and anthologies as well as enter comps, then Duotrope is a good deal too. But neither of these is essential, so don't worry if you'd rather not spend the money, or (like many writers) simply don't have any. If you do sign up to them then make sure to register for their newsletters, the Duotrope Weekly Wire and the Firstwriter Personal Alert Summary.

On-going comps

Here are on-going comps. Check each for submission guidelines and eligibility, as they vary quite a bit. Don't forget to add the ones for which you're eligible to your Competition Schedule document. Enter as many of these as you can:

Annual

- **Costa Book Awards**
  www.costabookawards.com/short-stories.aspx
- **The Sunday Times EFG Short Story Award**
  www.booktrust.org.uk/prizes/5/
- **BBC National Short Story Award**
  http://www.bbc.co.uk/programmes/b0079gw3
- **Wergle Flomp Humor Poetry Contest:**
  http://winningwriters.com/contests/wergle/we_guidelines.php#.UjoSGH_nJdw
- **The Swanezine Short Story Competition:**
  https://sites.google.com/site/swanezine/short-story-competition
- **Barton College Crucible: Poetry and Fiction**
  Competition: www.barton.edu/crucible/

- **James White Award Short Story Competition** (note: sci-fi and non-professional authors only): www.jameswhiteaward.com/
- **Jane Martin Poetry Prize** (note: check the eligibility criteria): www.girton.cam.ac.uk/jane-martin-poetry-prize
- **Writers & Artists: Killer Fiction - Crime & Thriller Competition:** www.writersandartists.co.uk/competitions
- **Short Tales contest** (note: micro/flash fiction with a large cash prize): www.museodelapalabra.com/en/short-tales-contest

Monthly, quarterly or thereabouts

- **Think Geek Techie Haiku** www.thinkgeek.com/haiku/?cpg=56231640&msg_id=56231640&et_rid=952558378&linkid=56231640_text
- **The Premises Mini-Contest** (note: short story on a given theme; see Chapter 4 for ways to approach competition themes.) http://onthepremises.com/current_contest.html

- **Creative Writing Ink:**
  http://creativewriting.ie/competitions-and-events/
- **Eric Hoffer Award for Short Prose**
  www.bestnewwriting.com/BNWsubmit.html
- **Blue Mountain Arts Biannual Poetry Card Contest:**
  www.sps.com/c_u+PV2qkA9iCLKAAo0IAkA/c_ut+1332109752/poetry/index.html
- **The Telegraph Travel Writing Competition:**
  www.telegraph.co.uk/travel/travel-writing-competition/
- **Blotterature Literary Magazine 50 for 50 words:**
  https://blotteratureliterarymagazine.submittable.com/submit
- **CampTrip Camping Writing Contest:**
  http://writingcontest.camptrip.com/
- **L. Ron Hubbard's Writers of the Future Contest:**
  www.writersofthefuture.com/Contest-Rules-Writers
- **Poem Pigeon Poetry Competition:**
  www.poempigeon.com/competition.php

- **Toasted Cheese Writing Contest:**
  http://tclj.toasted-cheese.com/contest.htm#amt
- **The Penn Cove Literary Arts Award:**
  (note: US-only)
  http://whidbeystudents.com/student-choice-contest/student-choice-contest-rules/
- **Unmanned Press Short of the Month:**
  http://www.unmannedpress.com/#!shortsubmissions/c12gv
- **The Spectator Competition:**
  (note: details of the competition are below the results of the previous contest.)
  http://www.spectator.co.uk/life/competition/

Your competition document/calendar should be shaping up nicely now! You've done most of the hard work to source comps already. Just quickly scan each newsletter when it arrives, and visit the websites once a month. That way you should keep a good number of competitions to enter each month - at least ten, and preferably twenty.

Finally, I put together a monthly listing of free writing competitions and calls for submission at:

- **www.compsandcalls.com**

Enter those comps! My Comps and Calls will give you a good few contests each month, along with calls for submission, all free, and all with easy electronic entry. It's updated on the first of every month.

If you don't have internet access, then do visit your local library where you can get it free, in most cases. Some libraries also run free courses in how to use the internet. If you really don't like the world of the web, however, then you can still find writing comps. Check the magazines you subscribe to - check the products you buy - check your newspapers (both local and national), and leaflets you find in shops. Your local library, if you are lucky enough to have one, will also have newspapers and magazines that will contain many competitions, some of them writing comps. Chapter 6 will be particularly useful to people in your situation. Ask your writer friends and your local writing groups if they know of any postal writing competitions. Most people are keen to help and will tell you if they can. Friends may print out entry forms to postal writing comps for you, if you ask nicely. But I do recommend becoming internet-savvy if you can, for many reasons.

Chapter 6
Comps that don't look like comps

In the last chapter I gave a list of places to find writing competitions and helpful advice. There is, however, another type of writing competition, one that hardly any writers bother to enter, even though they are well-qualified to enter and would stand a good chance of winning.

You know those competitions you sometimes see on cereal packets or in magazines? The ones that ask you to complete a sentence along the lines of, 'This brand of margarine makes me feel as if I've gone to heaven because....' in no more than twelve extra words. They are called slogan competitions and although competition professionals enter them, writers rarely do.

Some, of course consider this sort of thing beneath them. Such people might want to consider the fact that Sylvia Plath and Ted Hughes once spent weeks trying to think up Dole pineapple jingles in order to win a cash prize, and two more serious writers it would be hard to find. Most of the literati respect at least one of them, if not both! Many of our greatest writers (and greatest artists in various other media, come to that) have worked for money, and taken hopeful punts at commissions and any other sources of cash.

You need cash to live. Don't turn your nose up at an honest, if odd, way of earning some from your pen.

I must confess that this realisation is a recent one, so I haven't wins of this type listed in my 'Credentials' section - yet. But years ago I did enter one, just before I went to university, and I won six rucksacks and two pairs of trainers - ideal for student life! My winning slogan was silly, catchy and funny and I'm too embarrassed to write it down here, but hey - it got me the prize.

The other thing is that you stand a really good chance of winning. All those workshop exercises that you've done where you had to write tiny poems, all those short stories you wrote to a given theme - that work really pays off here. You are used to writing to themes and to order, and you might as well have a go, if it's free. Some competitions require proof of purchase - well, unless you buy the brand anyway, just ignore those.

How to find 'em

So where to find such comps? There's one simple answer to this - a website I've loved for years, and thanks to which I won many prizes in my general comping days: The Prizefinder.

- **www.theprizefinder.com**

Go and register there - it's free. Then scroll down to 'Creative Competitions'. Two of these are ideal for you: 'slogans' and 'writing'. Both will involve some kind of creative writing, which is your speciality.

Before you start creating, just check the rules - the winner may be drawn at random, in which case just write the first (clean) thing that comes into your head. Don't waste precious creative energy when you don't need to use it.

If the prize will not be drawn randomly, approach the comps as writing exercises. If you have read this book up to this point, then you know how to do that - you already have the skills you need. Yes, it can be really hard to find inspiration concerning a loaf of bread or a car manufacturer, but just think of aspects and stories - memorable times and places you've broken bread, the odd thing about cars that you always notice. You may be able to work them into a quirky or witty sentence. Look on them as haiku, or microfiction.

Remember the golden rule: if you have followed the guidelines and proofread your work properly, then you stand a chance, so submit your work.

When the contest results are announced, look and see what won - you will learn the sort of thing that catches judges' eyes. Like almost all aspects of writing, the ability to win competitions of this type can be developed and honed. It's unlikely, unless you get bitten by the comping bug, to be a steady source of income, but in odd moments it's worth having a go. In my comping days (not writing competitions - just prize draws) I used to win roughly 1 in 300 of the competitions that I entered. Add in any level of skill, such as a slogan or tie-breaker or any other form of creative writing, and the odds improve massively in your favour if you are literate and have writing skills. And it's such fun dreaming of the prizes...holidays, new kitchens, all those exotic things that few writers can afford.

Have a go, and enjoy it!

A quick update

Stop the press for this quick update! I've just won a trip to Rome by doing one of these. I had to describe my perfect moment in no more than fifty words. I didn't do anything spectacular, but just wrote an honest description of my perfect moment (a Devon beach and a Devon tea with my OH, if you must know!) but of course as writers, we express these things well. Imagine winning a free holiday by writing a fifty-word piece - I've just done that! So please don't decide too soon that these prizes aren't for you. Use your talents and get winning!

Chapter 7
I'm still waiting...

In 2011 I had a period of winning very little - nothing for a few months. At first I was annoyed with the various organisers who were ignoring my work, and then I blamed dumb luck. Then I remembered what constitutes the source of most writerly problems - the writer, i.e. me, in this case.

I had got sloppy. I was doing one edit and one proof on each poem, and it wasn't enough. I had become overconfident, too, and was no longer making such a concentrated effort with each piece I wrote. Nor was I spending enough time making sure that the piece I was entering was suited to the comp - I even skipped the reading of a few submission guidelines, which is a sure-fire way not to win.

There is some excuse for this - I was working hard on another project, and that was taking most of my focus. I was also having some serious health problems. If winning writing competitions is important to you, however, then you have to save some focus and concentration for that.

Waiting for the first win

Perhaps the worst time is when you're waiting for that very first win. At that point you don't have the affirmation of prior success, and it's understandably daunting when you enter and enter and enter and get nothing back. It's confidence-shaking, and you're bound to wonder if there's any point.

There are a few things to remember when this happens.

The first is something that I said in an earlier chapter: the ability to win writing competitions is a skill that you can learn, if you have basic writing ability. Remember that you are learning as you go along, becoming more familiar with competitions and their results, and finding out (in those judge's reports) why the things that won were chosen.

You are also getting used to the basic nuts and bolts of entry. This is a really useful skill, particularly if you want to submit your poems and short stories (and other work too, if you like) for publication. Most of us do want publication of some sort, and everything that you have been learning as you enter competitions - the courtesy, the attention to the rules, the writing exercises, the proofing - will stand you in the best stead when it comes to submitting your work.

There are also a few useful things that you can do to increase your chances of winning. Of these, the most important is: don't give up. DON'T GIVE UP. Do NOT, under ANY circumstances, give up.

Did I mention not quitting?

Here's one of my favourite writing quotes. It comes from Richard Bach, bestselling author:

"A professional writer is an amateur who didn't quit."

Yup. That's it in a nutshell.

At every stage of entering a competition, a number of writers will drop out. Some won't try to write anything for the comp - either it doesn't grab them, or they don't have the time because they are concentrating on something else, or whatever. Several will be bored by the guidelines and entry procedure and will quit at that point.

A large number will logic themselves out of entry: their writing isn't good enough; there's no point; or any number of reasons to stop the entry process. I mentioned this in Chapter 2.

Then there's this point - when you haven't won anything at all, and you're thinking that perhaps you never will.

Don't drop out now!

Difficult questions

For one thing - have you really done everything in this book?

I had a friend say, "I entered three competitions but didn't win anything, so I stopped."

I didn't win the first three comps I entered, either - but I carried on, and now have a large hatful of prizes.

How many have you entered? Ten or twenty isn't enough, as I said at the start. Certainly don't take the decision that your work isn't currently prizeworthy until you've entered many more than that. How many is up to you. But still don't give up - look at your work instead.

Is the spelling really perfect? Is the grammar correct? Have any clichés seeped unbidden into your work? Look at what the piece is saying or doing - has it been said or done a million times before?

I hope that you're reading as much poetry and/or fiction as possible. Some authors don't, in case it affects their writing - well, I tend to go with the opposite view. Reading feeds my writing, and the wider the reading, the better. The classics are of course excellent places to see how it's done, but do read other works too. Fay Weldon once said that any bestseller from any decade will tell us about the time it was written, and such books, even if terrible technically, can be very informative. I believe also that you are far more likely to find your own 'voice' by reading other people's.

The other thing that reading will do is to tell you whether your idea is original. I thought that the first story I wrote as an adult, in 2006, was brilliant: it was a retelling of Cinderella from the point of view of The Ugly Sisters. Little did I know (and that phrase is a cliché and should not make it into your work, unless used ironically) that 'my' idea had already been done to death (another cliché. It's so easy for them to creep in). Some submission guidelines expressly forbade the retelling of fairy tales via different characters, as I found out later when trying to get it published!

It's actually a well-written story - but it won't get published and it won't win prizes.

So - is your piece doing or saying or showing something that isn't exactly the same as the others?

Do go back over the chapters dealing with the Basics and Getting the Edge. Take your recent non-winners and go through the checklist with them. Then if they really are fine - enter them in another competition. Keep doing this with a piece until you are absolutely fed up of the thing - and then start submitting it for publication, which is slightly easier than winning competitions (see Chapter 9).

Are you really learning all that you can from your fellow writers? Have you met some at workshops, or made friends with any on Facebook (Napowrimo Sharing Groups on Facebook are very good for this)? For the most part, in my experience, writers are a friendly and helpful lot. There are a few unpleasant ones, of course, and there will be people you do and people you don't get on with. Chatting to the former will help you to learn and improve. Attitude is so important - my Facebook feed is a daily reminder of why some writers do, and some writers don't, achieve their goals. Luck and other things play their part too, I admit, but attitude is the one you can work on. I've seen some startlingly talented writers fail to achieve the publication and prizes they want because of their unpleasant personalities and refusal to learn anything or to take any kind of advice at all. I'm not recommending that you become a Pollyanna, cheerleading your way through your social life - just that you behave in a friendly and professional way and listen to the ideas of other writers, particularly if they offer you free constructive criticism.

When your friends click 'Like' and give you praise, that's wonderful, particularly if they say why they liked certain parts of a piece. This gives you much-needed confidence. But even more useful is the advice offered by other writers when looking at a piece. If a writer, particularly one you respect, says that they didn't really like a section of your piece and explains why in detail, you can learn not only about the piece but also about the writer's mentality.

An example: Dominic Berry, a fine, successful, full-time poet, was once going through an early poem of mine.

"How much are you attached to that 'and'?" he asked. That made me realise just how much attention one should be paying when editing, and how important the choice of even connective words can be.

So don't bridle when someone says something 'negative' about your poem, unless they're just pointlessly nasty and/or trolling. Learn from it if it strikes you as informative, thank them for the input and forget about it if it doesn't. Do save your early drafts though, in case you change your mind.

Do remember, when posting work, to keep the post private, available to selected friends only - otherwise it may count as published, and therefore become ineligible for many prizes and publications.

Next: when did you last try something really different with your work? I know several poets who are stuck in free verse autobiography loops. They write poems about I, I, I and the things that happened to them or what they think. Now some autobiographical free verse poems are superb, but please, please have a go at other forms and approaches. Or at least make that 'I' a black beetle, or a planet, or your worst enemy, occasionally, just to shake things up a bit.

How much are you writing? Are you making time for the writing of your poetry and fiction, and for the careful submission of your work?

Chapter 8
I've won! I've won! Now what?

If you haven't yet won anything, then skip this chapter. Come back to it when you have.

If you have won something - congratulations! That's wonderful news! I wrote this book in order to make that happen.

The first thing to do is to reply to the email telling you that you won. Keep it short, but explain in your own words how pleased and grateful you are. This makes the competition organiser happy too - they want to spread the joy. If you were informed by phone call then it can be hard to stay coherent, but as long as you are courteous then it won't matter too much.

Please remember to be gracious if you have won a 3rd place or runner-up prize. You won a prize! Brilliant! Don't say to the organiser, "Awww, I really wanted to win. I bet my story is as good as the winning one." For one thing it's rude, and for another, it's not easy to judge competitions. The majority of judges do their very best, but the decision is always a subjective one. Also, it's not a good mental attitude to sigh after a bigger prize when you have just won something.

There's a story about the author Joseph Heller being teased at a posh party for not earning much. A young financier was pointed out to him as earning ten times as much as Heller.

"But I have something that he'll never have," said Heller, and when he was disbelievingly asked what he could possibly have that the rich young man didn't have, he replied, "Enough."

Be glad that you got that runner-up prize, however small it is. Someone recognised your work as prizeworthy, and is giving you something, free, because of it. That is magnificent.

Caveats

One caveat here – do beware of letters or emails that say, 'You are a runner-up! Now if you just send us £50, we'll send you a copy of the magnificently-bound book that features your poem among others....'

There's an excellent list of contests that they suggest you avoid at Winning Writers:

- **https://winningwriters.com/the-best-free-literary-contests/contests-to-avoid**

I've been caught out by a couple of these myself. There's no shame in it - but just be a bit careful.

Don't be ashamed of coming first

And if you came first? Revel in it! This is your moment! You are queen of the bees, king of the hill, top of the pile! Of all the entries, the judges liked yours the best, and they are rewarding you for it! Even if the prize is just a certificate, you enjoy that moment. Tell all your friends. Don't go on and on about it, but let them know and let them know that you are happy. They will be happy for you.

Remember to thank the person who contacted you, and ask them to thank everyone involved. It is permissible to ask when your prize will arrive, and I suggest that you do this. Whatever they say - whether it's coming in a week or month, say, "Thank you! How exciting!" or something similar, and leave it at that for now.

Then sit and wait for your prize.

Sometimes a prize doesn't arrive. This is actually happening to me as I write this - the sponsor of a competition hasn't yet sent the cheque out, though the competition results were published over a month ago. This is why you ask the organiser when the prize might arrive - so that you can query when it doesn't. If you forgot to ask (or couldn't face asking) at the time, send a polite query email about a month after the competition results were announced. It's embarrassing to do this, and one of the least nice parts about being a prizewinner, but you won the prize fair and square and you are entitled to it. Also, the organisers will want to know if the sponsor isn't providing what they promised.

Usually, however, your prize will arrive soon after the announcement, and again - enjoy it! If it's a book, smell that new-book-smell, and enjoy reading something that you might not otherwise have chosen. If it's a certificate, keep it in a special box for publications and certificates and articles about you and such delights. I used to refer to mine as my 'vanity box' until it was pointed out to me that I was adding negative connotations to a happy thing. You work hard at your writing and you have earned everything in your Success Box. That's what I call mine now, though of course you may want to find a different name. Make it a positive one, though.

If the prize is cash - yay! You may need it for household expenses or the paying of debts, or you may wish to spend some. I beg you, however, to spend at least a little on something lovely for yourself, as a treat. It can be something practical - with one of my wins I bought a nice crockery set, so that my writing paid for us to eat from attractive plates and bowls. Or it can be as frivolous as you like - hair accessories, a restaurant meal, or just a chocolate bar if the cash is a tiny amount. But you enjoy every bite of that bar. It's a special bar. And you can honestly tell people that your writing put food on your table, even if it was only once!

Basically, you've achieved something special. Not many people win writing competitions. You slaved over a hot computer and you did it! You won! You are BRILLIANT! Congratulations!

No doubt you will not win others that you have entered, and if you submit to magazines and anthologies too then you will inevitably get rejections. Time passes, and the glow wears off. Well - maybe you'll win another comp soon. And even if you don't, no one can take that achievement away from you. You are a winner.

Standing on ceremony

Some competitions have award ceremonies. This may sound intimidating - will you have to dress up posh, like at the Oscars? Do try to find photos of previous award ceremonies for that comp, if possible, so that you have an idea what to wear. If there's no info, or you've won or been placed in the inaugural competition, then I have two pieces of advice re. dress, and which one you take will depend on your personality.

The safe thing to do is to dress almost formally but not quite - a long-ish but not ankle-length skirt with a smart-but-not-glitzy top, or an ordinary suit with a casual shirt (and a tie in your pocket just in case).

The second option is to wear whatever the hell you like - the thing you love that expresses you perfectly, and will make you happy to wear it. I have one friend who wears nothing but ballgowns, because she likes them best of all clothes - to work, for walks, to parties....and she looks great. I have another who dresses in either Victorian or Regency dress most of the time. She too looks utterly fantastic. I have another friend who wears jeans and check shirts for every occasion, because that's what she likes best and it's what reflects her personality and politics. Good for her!

If you dare - and why not? - then wear whatever will make you happiest. Obviously, if dressing up will make you feel self-conscious or unhappy, then don't do it. Ditto dressing down.

The idea is to enjoy your award ceremony as much as you possibly can, and whether that means blending in or standing out is up to you, if there's no dress code on the invitation. If it really is an issue, then ask the organiser - s/he won't mind.

Be the professional you are

If you are invited to an award ceremony or reading, then be professional there too, just as you were when you entered the competition. If you can't go, let the organisers know in plenty of time and express your regrets. If you go, then arrive on time and be polite to everyone there. Support the other performers with your attention during their readings and your applause afterwards, even if they weren't brilliant. You don't know them or what they might have been through to get to this point, so give them the benefit of the doubt and be supportive. Applaud! Smile, and mean it!

Turn your phone off! Follow the organiser's instructions and do not hog the stage or mutter self-deprecations or perform a piece that you haven't practised. Respect your audience. Do not do an introduction that explains the piece or is longer than the piece.

There are various articles on the internet about what to do and not to do when performing spoken word or poetry - most of the rules apply to award ceremonies too, so I suggest reading some.

Try as hard as possible not to get drunk. I know - it's tempting. But you want to remember the evening, don't you? If you must let your hair down then at least do it towards the end, so that you don't spoil anyone else's night, by throwing up during their acceptance speech, for instance. Not cool.

As always, be professional, be polite, and enjoy yourself.

So what now? Carry on entering writing comps, of course! I promise you that the fun of entering and winning doesn't wear off.

Is there a next step? That depends on you and your preferences. See my suggestions in Chapter 9.

Chapter 9
What next?

So you've mastered the techniques in this book and you have a prize or two under your belt. Excellent work! Perhaps you'd like to move on to the next stage - well, what is the next stage?

There are several possibilities now, and which you choose is up to you.

Submitting

One I hope you will choose is to submit your work to magazines and anthologies. For one thing, some of these pay, so that it's like winning a small competition. Some offer free copies too, which is another sort of prize. All the things you have learned from this book will help you to get published and paid for your work.

The first step is to find places to submit. Here are some useful links:

- **Cathy's Comps and Calls**
  (note: this is my website. Just submit to the 'Calls' as well as entering the 'Comps'!)
  http://compsandcalls.com
- **Poetry Library Southbank Centre:**
  www.poetrylibrary.org.uk/magazines/magazines
- **Writing Career:**
  writingcareer.com
- **New Pages:**
  www.newpages.com/classifieds/calls-for-submissions
- **Every Writer:**
  www.everywritersresource.com/literarymagazines/category/print-magazineonline-submissions/
- **Freelance Writing:**
  www.freelancewriting.com/freelancejobs/writing career-call-for-submissions.php
- **Funds for Writers:**
  (note: one of the best)
  www.fundsforwriters.com/markets/

- **JBWB Writers Markets:** http://jbwb.co.uk/markets.html
- **Lambda Literary**: www.lambdaliterary.org/category/subs/

There are, of course, many, many more. These are just examples of some sites that I have used to find places to send my work. Never, ever pay a submission fee - that's like vanity publishing, only without the publishing!

Another technique you can use, and it's very useful if you don't have internet access, is to look at a book of short stories or poems and check the acknowledgements. The places (usually litmags) that first published the pieces might publish yours, too. Most libraries have a reference copy of "The Writers' and Artists' Yearbook" in which you should be able to find postal addresses or phone numbers for the various litmags or periodicals.

Good luck and as always, have fun and enjoy it. Submit dozens of pieces to different places for the maximum chance of success. Avoid the litmags that charge submission fees!

Book publication

After some success with publication, you may even be able to pitch a novel, poetry or short story collection to a publisher and have a Whole Proper Book published. For an aspiring writer, there is no experience quite like it.

Forgive me for the plugs, but I've had two full poetry collections published so far, and neither of them was self-published (though I did marry one of the publishers in the end - well, how could I resist?): *Contains Strong Language and Scenes of a Sexual Nature* (Puppywolf, 2010) and *Look at All the Women* (Mother's Milk, 2014). Both have lists of acknowledgements in which you may be able to find potential markets for your work, particularly my most recent collection, from which most poems had been previously published.

Performing

Do you secretly long to be applauded on stage, or are you terrified of the idea? Or both?! Either way, I hope you'll have a go at it. Have a look in your local event listings for Spoken Word/Poetry events, and attend them. If you have a poem that reads well, then sign up for the open mic and have a go. You have nothing to lose at all - hosts will always be kind if you explain that it's your first time, and audiences tend to be sympathetic. Pay attention to the other acts, and you'll see what works and what doesn't. Applaud the other performers and as always, be courteous.

I have known people who were scared to death at the thought of performing, but who have now been bitten by the bug and adore it. Some have gone on to community or theatre groups and perform regularly. Please do consider giving this a try!

There are some simple things you can do to make the experience less nerve-racking, and more likely to please your audience.

Firstly, match your poem(s) to the event. If the event is 'Poetry and Pies' at your local pub, then your acrostic sonnet crown exploring the more esoteric aspects of Marcusian theory may not be a good choice. Your set of limericks about cheese and pickle sandwiches, or your free verse comic poem about sex, may go down a treat though. Conversely, at your local arts centre or library, your more formal poems may be appreciated.

Secondly, practise your poems! So many people don't bother, and it shows. Just read each one through a loud at home a couple of times. This also gives you the chance to time them - if the open mic slot is three minutes long then DON'T exceed it. Remember to practise with a microphone - i.e. a hairbrush or a toothpaste tube or whatever - an inch from your mouth throughout the reading.

Before the performance: make sure that your poems are typed or written clearly, and that you have the pages in the right order. Do not rely on electronic devices - they are too unreliable.

When you are introduced, take the time to take a deep, long breath and let it out. Then smile and walk to the mic (or the performance area if there is no mic). Deep breath again - and then read the poems.

Do not be tempted to do a long, unrehearsed intro. This spoils many performances. The performer may have practised his or her poems, but launches into a ramble that explains the whole poem and leaves nothing for it to do. If you must introduce your poem, make it a sentence or two at most - and rehearse it beforehand, just as you rehearsed the actual poems.

Do not get drunk. If you like a drink, then one will help to relax you, but don't overdo it.

If you lose your place (I wouldn't advise memorising your poems until you are comfortable with performing) then just stop and find it again. Don't worry - it happens. No one will mind.

This is a big one and some very good performers forget it or don't care for it, for some unimaginable reason - when you finish a piece, indicate it in some way so that the audience knows to clap. I nod and say, 'thank you', for example. Some performers nod and smile. Others do nothing, and then wonder why the audience doesn't seem to like them. The reason that the audience isn't clapping is that they don't know whether or not the poem is finished, or whether you have just paused dramatically, and they don't want to get it wrong. Give a little help.

All this said - enjoy yourself! Performing to and gelling with an audience are delightful and addictive. If you do all the above things then you will be behaving as a professional and should be able, after a few goes, to relax a bit and enjoy it.

I always get terrible nerves - until I'm actually onstage. Then I love it to bits. It's draining, but I wouldn't miss it for anything.

Entry fees

Some entry fees are ridiculous. £40? $75?! Don't enter those! Once you've got the hang of entering writing comps and the odd bit of confidence going, start entering the ones with sensible fees, if you can afford it. There are many of these, and you can find them at most of the links I listed in Chapter 1. Prices range from £1 upwards, so if you do have a little disposable income and a good body of work, why not have a go? All the same techniques still apply. In the more prestigious and high-paying comps you'll be up against the professionals, but so what? If you've won writing competitions and/or had work published, then you are a professional writer too. Remember not to talk yourself into imaginary limits, and logic yourself out of a perfectly valid entry. When you win the bigger competitions you'll get publicity for your writing projects, too, which can help sales and also help you to meet more people from the writing community.

When I won the Bulwer-Lytton Fiction Prize in 2012, I was featured in many newspapers, including in the USA. I also gave a radio interview - there I was, knees knocking nervously in my living room in Manchester, UK, while on the air to 700,000 listeners in America! The resulting sales sent my first poetry book into profit, and the whole experience was marvellous. I also got to swap emails with the other winners, who were lovely. This was free to enter, actually, but just a bit of publicity can help enormously with sales.

So spend a little cash (not too much, please!) and have some fun.

Community Projects, qualifications and careers

I know writers who go into prisons; I know other writers who visit schools. I know writers who work with theatre groups; I've worked with dancers and artists. Some of my friends have obtained degrees or other qualifications in creative writing, and some have become professional creative writing teachers. Several friends run workshops of various kinds, and do gig tours and festivals. Some are journalists, and their comp training in writing on given themes to deadlines has been invaluable.

Really, there are opportunities of all kinds, and don't miss out on the ones that might suit you. All these things can be challenging and will develop your writing, and some of them may make you money and even provide a full-time living. As your writing progresses and you have more and more success and experience, remember to give something back and pass your skills on to the writing community, and perhaps to foster a love of writing in those who up to now have had too little confidence to try.

Some of us become full-time writers. For some of us, writing is our life, our main activity. And most of us are happier than we've ever been before.

Whatever you choose don't forget to keep entering those writing competitions! Those little nuggets of free inspiration and cash are still there waiting for you to enter. They can make a nice little (or not so little!) addition to your income, as well as being great fun. So don't forget everything you've learned in this book, and keep winning! And please, please keep enjoying your writing. The very best of luck.

Cathy x

Appendix A: Examples of winning poems and stories

So how do I do it? I've tried to answer that in this book, of course, but here's some of my winning work for further study. After each I'll discuss what work went into it, and why it won.

I'll start with my most reprinted poem: *The Poetry Diet,* which won the Marple Humorous Poetry Prize in

2010 and has been reprinted in various places, as well as being read out on BBC Radio 4's *Poetry Please.*

Poetry: The Poetry Diet –
Drop a Stanza in Just Two Weeks!

Breakfast is blank verse spread with ballads
Or a bowl of elegy and a boiled ode.

For lunch, try a rondelet with herbs such as cento.
Follow with a lay if liked,
Sweetened artificially if necessary.
Vary your cinquains and quatrains
According to season.

For dinner a well-grilled villanelle
With a simple side sonnet and a little steamed prose.
Do beware of prose. It can be hard to stop.
Make sure to keep crunchy acrostics to hand.

For snacks, try haiku.
They're surprisingly meaty
And will satisfy.

Free verse is unlimited.

Drink at least eight couplets a day,
And up to three glasses of freshly-squeezed phrases.

When tempted by fizzy limericks,
Chewy clerihews, chocolate epics and sweet lyrics,

Visualise yourself as a sexy sestina
Rather than doughy doggerel.
This poem is scientifically proven
And has been approved by dactyls
And other members of the metrical profession.
It really, really works.

So that's the poem - I hope that you enjoyed it! I talked to the judge later, who I met her at the performance in Marple that was part of the prize, along with a very welcome £125. Her name is Joyce Reed, and I look up to her as a poet - her poetry has that mature, considered yet sometimes playful air that I find beguiling in verse.

Anyway, she was lovely, and I asked her why she'd picked my poem. Joyce explained that it was fun but also well-edited. It didn't have wasted lines but kept to its theme.

Another editor said that it really captured the irritatingly breezy tone of diet books.

I often find that a poem you really have fun writing will turn out well, though one has to edit extra carefully. Sometimes the lines that please the writer most won't appeal to a general audience or anyone who doesn't know your references.

My TIP based on this win: Have fun while you write. Every once in a while, write something that gives you enormous pleasure. Then edit with a cool eye.

Now let's look at *Timewalker and the Riddle,* which won the MR Jordan Short Story Competition in 2013. This brought me $50 and taught me a few lessons:

Fiction: Timewalker and the Riddle

If like myself you're a time traveller, or timewalker as we tend to call ourselves, then you'll know already the most important pieces of wisdom on the subject: wear comfortable shoes and socks, and clutch a roll of loo paper hard when you feel the pull. You've no idea how many times don't contain these three important things.

Of course that's when you're pulled by magic, invocation or something of that nature, and get to wear the clothes you had on and take the objects you are holding. If technology brings you, then the chances are you'll stumble into the Arrival Time naked and covered in some sciency kind of goo. You know the sort of thing. This can be embarrassing when they're expecting a muscular hero; but unfortunately, people usually get what they've specified, regardless of looks, and from time to time that's me – forty, fat and female, and quite cheerful about it.

Oh, a couple more pieces of advice – if the magic isn't quite strong enough to start you timewalking, don't help. They need to be strong enough to send you back as well, remember, and after performing whatever it is they think they need, you may be in no shape to assist. And the other piece of advice – avoid all puzzles and riddles. If these form part of your task, refuse. It's that simple. Just say no.

As I'm sure you've guessed, these are all things that I've learned by experience, some of which I am about to share with you, hopefully for your edification.

Sadly, the people doing the calling had no problems calling me strongly enough. If only! No, they had no problems, and it wasn't so much a timewalk as a few seconds of mad sprinting into what turned out to be, um, somethingth century Russia. I never found out the exact date – well if it's the pre-newspaper era then how does one tell? - but it was in the time of the Tsars, as I found out later, and it was Spring. Melting snow, birds hopefully tweeting, little flowers, all that. Very pretty, and so were the people. Bright long skirts, headscarves, all hand made of course, as was the 'peasant' furniture of beautifully carved wood, probably priceless in my hometime. We were at an inn in a small village square.

I began as I usually do, 'Hi there, I'm the Timewalker. What year is it please, where am I, and what do you want me to do?'

At which point they all began speaking in what sounded like Russian, and I understood nothing. Then a teenage girl stepped forward.

I say teenage; somehow the concept of the teenager doesn't fit various types of young person. To me, she was a sharp young woman. To her father, she was probably his lovely clever little girl. She had dark hair and black, bird-quick eyes; she looked strong rather than shapely and had a decided look about the mouth, which I liked. She gazed at me without fear or awe but with great curiosity, which I also liked.

"Good day," she said in gorgeously accented English, "I am the only one to speak English in this village. You are in Russia. I am known as the Clever Little Girl."

"Pleased to meet you," I said cheerfully, and sat down on one of the wooden chairs.

The villagers showed great sense by providing the pair of us with food (dark, flavoursome bread, pickles, fresh vegetables; a divine salad; and some meat which I refused. I'm trying to cut down my red meat consumption) and drink - sweet tea or beer. I had both.

"This is nice," I remarked. "So, what do you want of me?"

"We would like you to solve a riddle," answered the Clever Little Girl.

"Um, I'm not great at riddles," I said uncertainly, never having been asked to do this before and having little experience of riddles outside the pages of Tolkien.

"That doesn't matter," said the CLG with a dismissive wave of her hand and a pout. "The riddle is easy, and you have plenty of time to solve it."

"If it's easy, why don't you solve it yourself?" I asked, reasonably enough, I thought.

The CLG explained.

"The Tsar has set the riddle. He was told by a magician that he must marry the one who can solve the riddle. I have no wish to marry him, or anyone for that matter. I wish to be educated, and to travel, before choosing a husband, if I do so at all. And he certainly won't be a great lout who plays god and rules with a rod of iron! To which end, if no one solves the riddle, our charming Tsar will start burning villages and making war and so on, as this fool magician has told him that his happiness and reign are dependent on getting it solved. So someone must solve it - but no one has. Except me — and I won't do it!"

"I see," I said, and thought for a bit.

"I don't want to marry the Tsar either," I said firmly.

"I've thought of that," said the CLG. 'You can just go through with the ceremony, and then we can send you back to your time and place."

"As long as you do..."

"I give my word."

Famous last words. I sighed, and decided to trust her.

"OK, as long as you promise no honeymoon on the sly. And if you don't come through, I can always tell the Tsar the secret – that you solved the riddle first, not me. What is the riddle?"

"You have to turn up at the palace neither mounted nor on foot, neither eating nor fasting, neither clothed nor naked, neither alone nor attended, and neither speaking not silent."

"Oh for gooodness' sake. How childish."

"Magicians are like that," sighed the girl.

"So I have to express a load of contradictions. Oh I HATE this."

"But you will do it?"

"If I can," I said rather feebly.

"I have thought of that too," smiled the horribly efficient CLG. "You are from the future, are you not? So you must have many books, many documents, and the accumulated knowledge of centuries."

"And the accumulated stupidity, but yes, go on," I said. "I don't suppose you'll just tell me the answer?"

"I can't do that or the Tsar might hear of it and demand to marry me. No, you must do it. We'll send you back to your time, you can find the answer, and then we'll pull you back."

"That's not been done before that I know of," I said thoughtfully. "You can really send me back and forth like that?"

"We are a very strong people," said that determined mouth, "Especially me."

"I'm beginning to see that," I muttered.

"So we'll send you home now. You'll have about a day to find the answer, and another to prepare it. Then we'll pull you back, just outside the Palace."

"Terrific," I sulked. "I'm so glad. May I take one of these chairs with me?"

–

Only a few seconds. Well, hundreds of years, but it felt like a few seconds as I stumbled rather than walked through time, clutching my soon-to-be-antique chair tightly. They were good at this.

Usually when I get home after a timewalk I'm happy and relaxed. I breathe a sigh of relief that I'm home and that the event, whatever it was, is closed. Naturally it was different this time. I checked the clock, thought about the riddle, and began to panic. Then I ate the contents of my fridge and went to bed. Well, you can't solve riddles tired, anxious and on an empty stomach.

The next morning I began my research. Do you remember research? One sometimes sees it in old films. Information is needed, so one invites a professor to tea. After three hours of buns and banalities, one is given the facts one had hoped for. Or one has to search for hours or days, accompanied by creepy music in a dusty, dirty library of rare and ancient volumes. My research was rather different. That sounds quite impressive; what I actually mean, of course, is that I turned my computer on, and typed 'riddles' into a search engine.

What am I? I am the size of a castle but lighter than air, and a thousand men and their horses can't move me.

I decided to try to solve this, as it might help my mind get into the right groove to solve my riddle. Hmm. So it's something big, but light. A cloud? Why a thousand men? Is the number significant? What have the horses got to do with it? What can't horses move? An opinion?

Ten furious minutes later, I checked the answer.

I am the shadow of the castle.

Now come on. If the thousand men and their horses destroyed the castle, then the shadow would be destroyed too. In fact a cloud passing over the sun can destroy it, as can the coming of night. And light? How is a shadow light or heavy? Can shadows be weighed?

I simmered down and tried another.

How many letters are there in the alphabet?

Depends which alphabet, doesn't it? What a ridiculous question to ask unless a context is given.

The answer:

There are 11 letters in 'the alphabet'!

Well if you had punctuated it correctly the first time, I could have answered the question correctly. Punctuating poorly to cause ambiguity isn't riddling, it's just annoying. Or is that allowed in Riddledom?

And so on through various circles of riddle hell. I found the answer in the end by checking a mixture of Russian history and some fairytales. I remembered the CLG's words: "You have to turn up at the palace neither mounted nor on foot, neither eating nor fasting, neither clothed nor naked, neither alone nor attended, and neither speaking not silent."

– and I looked up various bits of that until I found it.

Originally it was a Norse fairy tale, apparently, which found its way across Europe in various forms before reaching Russia. The heroine rode on a goat with one foot trailing on the ground, she sang, nibbling an onion, wearing a fishing net, with a bird on her shoulder. The magician had obviously heard the story and decided it was a good one to tease his patron with – when the villages failed, the 'magician' could explain the solution and look really clever.

Which was all fine and dandy, but I had hardly any time yet in which to procure these things. Fishing nets in a landlocked city? And who does same-day-delivery of goats? Not even online shops could oblige.

–

A few hours later I was ready and waiting for the pull. As I felt it I braced myself and clutched all the necessary items to me; and then came the fast steps through time, and there I was, outside what looked like a new palace near some marshland. A richly-dressed bloke stood there with sundry attendants. He saw me, and began to cross himself while uttering what looked and sounded like desperate prayers. The attendants' mouths dropped open and they too began to pray. A little extreme, I thought, but then I suppose that they hadn't seen a spectacle quite like the one I presented, before. Imagine it:

I was wearing a PVC peephole bra and matching crotchless knickers (which had been very hard to find in a large enough size), pushing myself along on a little scooter, with a robot dog beside me, while I sipped a diet shake and gargled noisily with it.

I thought that was pretty good. The assembled villagers did too after the initial shock, and applauded me loudly, the CLG laughing to herself.

"Come on," I said to the Tsar. "Let's get married then."

It is to his eternal credit that he did not faint.

—

The CLG came with us and did all the translation, thankfully. It was all taken care of. The Tsar, who had gibbered somewhat and expressed some distaste for the union, got a stiff talking-to from the CLG.

"Now listen," she said. "You started all this nonsense by listening to that idiot magician. And if you don't marry her, then every time something bad happens you'll blame it on not fulfilling your side of the bargain. But don't worry, she's as reluctant as you are. Just go through with the ceremony, then pretend that she's gone to a nunnery or something, and we'll send her back to her, er, village. You'll have fulfilled the terms of the riddle, and I suggest that after this you send away that magician. You'll have enough problems as Tsar without this sort of nonsense."

After that it was all utterly gorgeous. I got to wear a fabulous dress (all hand-done embroidery with little brilliants and lots of floaty skirt), and jewellery that was probably real (I had hoped to take some back to my hometime, but sadly I had to give it all back after the ceremony) and walk up the aisle of a posh church and say things in Russian that the CLG, my bridesmaid, whispered to me. It was great, like being in a movie. She and I smiled at each other. I kept her secret about solving the riddle, and she kept mine about being from the future. It seemed fair.

After the ceremony and an enormous meal, some maids came and took all the finery away and dressed me in a petticoat thingy, all giggling away like nutters. I think they were preparing me to lose my virginity, in which case they were in one sense hundreds of years too early, and in another sense very, very late. Just as I was starting to curse the CLG and her promise to return me, I timewalked and fell straight into my own time.

Ah, the relief. Ah, the joy. I had done the Task and was alive. And what had I gained? Well, I'd had a fantastic wedding day without having to put up with a husband afterwards. I'd saved the CLG from marriage with a fool – he had decided to build a city on a swamp, apparently. There was also the carved chair, which I had sent to an antique-dealing friend for appraisal. The following day I received this note from him:

'Various factors, such as the condition of the wood and the wear of the edges, lead me to believe that it was made very recently. It is a likeable enough peasant chair, but worthless as it is so new.'

– which is the other thing I meant to tell you. Stick to jewellery and ceramics when bringing back souvenirs – they're the only sure things. The rest of the antiques market is a riddle. [ENDS]

So here are the three lessons I learned from this: firstly, just because a contest is free, doesn't mean that it will get loads of entries. This one got just twenty! And secondly, guess how many entries followed all the submission guidelines? Just one - mine. Thirdly: the person who won second place queried and complained and did various things afterwards - with the competition organiser, who discussed his response on her blog. It taught me not to do that...

So here are my TIPS based on that experience: ALWAYS follow the guidelines. Many people won't, which makes it much easier for the judge. Don't talk yourself out of entering. And don't question the results - they're unlikely to change.

Here's a poem that has won two competitions:

Poetry: I Want One

Some facet of brakes or wheels strikes sparks
from the cobbles and the boy whoops and laughs
as his mother bumps the wheelchair along.
"Like a fairground ride!" she beams at me
and I smile back, doing my crutches-waltz

over the uneven stones, each unique like faces
or fingerprints, and the gentle moss between.

The sound and feel of crutch and feet:
clack-thud on the cobbles, silent softness
on moss, transmitted up to my arms.
The wheelchair sounds like a zipwire or train.

A girl, about six, is being dragged along by
her mother, her little legs reluctant. She looks
at the wheeling laughing boy in his sparking
chariot and tugs at her mother's hand: "Mom!
Look, Mom! See that? I want one! I want one!"

Although the event described in the poem is fictional, it stems from my experiences as a disabled person and my affection for Manchester cobbles, which are increasingly rare but much loved. I wrote it to the prompt of the first competition, which was the Creative Futures Literary Award in 2013: Spark. I was thinking about sparks and then of the irons that were once used to sole clogs (one of my first jobs was in a shop called Clogs and Wellies, and I know a fair amount about clogs). These iron soles used to strike sparks from the stone cobbles, and it struck me that the metal parts on a wheelchair might do the same. Now I know that this is poetic licence to a degree - usually only rubber tyres come into contact with the ground - but I liked the idea, and it also fitted with my notion of wheelchairs as chariots. Imagine the chariot race in the film *Ben Hur* done with wheelchairs! Fabulous.

So I entered it and won the gold award, which was delightful.

Then in 2014 I saw that Pen 2 Paper, the Coalition of Texans with Disabilities, were running a poetry competition for poems reflecting the disabled experience. I checked the rules carefully, and they didn't include the rule that one often sees: 'No poems must have been entered in or won another competition'. So I entered I Want One again, and it won! I was very pleased and grateful.

Is it ethical to win two contests with the same poem? Long after both competitions, I found myself discussing this with my writer friends. One person said that it prevented judges from being impartial, though I think that with the smaller comps the judge is unlikely to have seen the poem before. Another said that poems were like racehorses and can be raced more than once! After all, we're usually paid for initial publication in a magazine, and then again with royalties when the poem is part of a collection.

As always, it's up to you.

So here's my TIP from this experience: just because you're writing to a given theme for a competition, doesn't mean that you can't write passionately, joyfully and imaginatively (I'm not sure that I achieved all that, but I tried).

One-liners

I'm going to end this appendix with the single sentence that won me the Bulwer-Lytton Fiction Prize in 2012. This is a prize for the bad first sentence of a novel that hasn't been written - the entrants simply imagine how a terrible opening sentence might go:

As he told her that he loved her she gazed into his eyes, wondering, as she noted the infestation of eyelash mites, the tiny deodicids burrowing into his follicles to eat the greasy sebum therein, each female laying up to 25 eggs in a single follicle, causing inflammation, whether the eyes are truly the windows of the soul; and, if so, his soul needed regrouting.

Horrible, isn't it?! I'd heard recently about eyelash mites, and I couldn't get the images out of my head.

My TIP: if you have an image stuck in your mind, then run with it. Try it in different contexts and forms. If it's really vivid to you, then you may be able to transfer that to your work.

Tips from my experience as a judge

I've had quite a bit of judging experience now, both poetry and fiction, and one point I'll make is that for some reason, any fiction contest will be inundated with entries full of murder and knives and grim people cleverly poisoning their spouses. I'm not saying that such stories are bad - just that after the fiftieth, a story on the same theme will have to do an awful lot to ignite the judge's interest.

There are similar 'seen too often' themes in poetry. Occasionally there'll be a real gem from these categories, and I don't want to proscribe anyone's writing, but if your poem is on one of these themes then it may have to work that bit harder:

- Death/dementia/cancer has taken you away
- You're dead and I miss you
- I'm going through your possessions and I miss you
- We're getting divorced and it's your fault
- I'm going to kill you and you aren't expecting it
- She's been raped/killed and she's so pretty in her flimsy clothes
- I'm alone and sad. When will I meet my fantasy lover?
- The world is a dark, sick, putrefying sort of place
- I'm angry about politics and saying so with every cliché in the book
- I'm writing a poem about writing a poem
- We're breaking up and it's poignant

- Everyone should cheer up and stop being sad
- He died in war. War is bad.

Many of these are genuine, moving, human experiences and I don't want to belittle those experiences. Much of the poetry that results, however, isn't good, and there's an awful lot of it. It can be hard to get even your fine poem noticed in the crowd.

Some of these turn up regularly in fiction too, but there's some variety. Here are some fiction themes that I've seen too often:

- God/aliens decide(s) that humanity is too corrupt and destroys it
- I'm going through your possessions and I miss you
- We're getting divorced and it's your fault
- I'm going to kill you and you aren't expecting it
- I've killed you and I'm going to get away with it
- The characters and plot are a hanger for my political point
- We're breaking up and it's poignant
- It was all a dream, or in an insane narrator's mind.

If you write science fiction or fantasy stories then you may well benefit from reading Strange Horizons' list of themes seen too often, here:

- **www.strangehorizons.com/guidelines/fiction-common.shtml**

There's a fantastic list of phrases and clichés used too often in poetry here:

- **www.poetrysoup.com/poetry_resources/poetry_cliches.aspx**

Please, please write whatever you like. But if you plan to enter a competition, just be aware of what may not work unless it really is outstanding.

Appendix B
Layout and editing on a computer

Publishers sometimes demand your work be laid out a certain way to make it easier to read and annotate, especially if you're submitting printed versions. Some may specify the dreaded William Shunn format (see www.shunn.net/format/story.html) and here's how to go about setting up its key characteristics in Microsoft Word. Afterwards I take the opportunity to discuss briefly what other features of Word an editor might use when working with you once a piece has been accepted.

Font and lines

Let's start with the font, which is perhaps easiest. To switch the font in a document globally, highlight all of it either using the mouse, or by tapping Ctrl+A. Then make a choice from the font dropdown list on the Home ribbon. Shunn recommends either Times New Roman or Courier New. Don't use anything else – it runs the risk of irritating the editor.

To switch to double-line spacing, right-click any of the text while it is still highlighted, and select Paragraph from the menu that appears. In the dialog box that appears, select Double from the Line Spacing dropdown list.

Headers

Shunn suggests adding a header to each page with your name, the title of the piece, and page number. To do so, click Insert on the menu, then the Header entry on the ribbon (on some versions of Word you might need to click the View menu). You'll see various suggested styles but we want none of these. Instead, click simply Edit Header near the bottom of the list. Type your name, then a slash, then the name of the piece, then a slash. Finally, click the Page Number icon at the left of the ribbon, then from the pop-out menu select Current Position, then Plain Number. Don't forget to switch the font for the header to either Courier

New or Times New Roman, as mentioned earlier. To right-justify the text, tap Ctrl+R.

Once done, click the Close Header and Footer button on the ribbon.

Italics and bold

Shunn recommends using underline instead of italics, so editors can't miss the emphasis. That is, format your text like this:

`John was very angry.`

— rather than —

`John was very angry.`

Automatically swapping one for the other requires guru skills, although you can use the search function to find italic text, which you can then manually switch to underlining (highlight it, then tap Ctrl+I followed by Ctrl+U). To search for italics, click Home on the menu, then the small down arrow next to Find at the right of the ribbon. Select Advanced Find, and then in the dialog that appears, click the More button. Click the Format button, and then select Font in the menu that appears. You'll see the usual fonts dialog box but you can ignore most of it. Instead, just select the Italic style, then click OK. Leaving the Find What box empty, you can click the Find Next button to jump to each example of italics text.

Working with editors

There's a handful of advanced features that you might be asked to use if you're working with an editor on a document. Arguably the most useful is Track Changes, which as its name suggests lets you see deletions or additions made to a document. It can be activated by clicking Review on the menu, then the Track Changes button on the ribbon.

Each addition now made will appear in a different colour and be underlined (with a different colour for each person who makes the edit), while each deletion will be struck through. Because having deletions stick around can make things confusing, you can switch to having the deletions shown in annotation balloons which appear alongside the document - click Show Markup alongside the Track Changes button, then Balloons > Show Revisions in Balloons.

To see who made an edit, hover the mouse over it and within a few seconds their name, and the date and time of the annotation will appear. You can also right-click an edit to choose whether to accept or reject it, which will make it permanent and remove the annotation.

Your editor might also use comment balloons to make suggestions. These will appear at the right of the text, with the author's name added to them. You can insert your own comment balloon by clicking Review on the menu, then the New Comment button, after first highlighting text you want the comment to refer to.

Another way to track the edits made to a document is to use Word's Compare feature, by which you can compare the current version of the document against an earlier draft and view any deletions or annotations in the same way as described above. To do so, click Review on the menu, then the Compare icon on the toolbar. Then select the first option in the menu: Compare Two Versions Of A Document. In the dialog box that appears, click the small folder icon on the left to select the older draft from your hard disk. Then click the folder icon on the right of the dialog box and select the latest draft. Once you click OK a new document will be generated, which you'll see in the middle of the screen, and the older and newer documents will be at the right. You can once again go through and right-click each edit to accept or reject them, and can then save this new document in the usual way as the latest draft.

50635220R00080

Made in the USA
San Bernardino, CA
28 June 2017